4OP

SCOTLAND'S CONSTITUTION

Edited by
ROBBIE MOFFAT
Illustrated by
MATTHEW McKENNA

Moffat & Co. Publishing,The Quadrangle,Ruchill St, Glasgow G20 9PX

Library Cataloguing in Publication Data

Moffat, Robbie, ed

Scotland's Constitution

1. Law   I. 344.110223 CON

ISBN 0 907282 20 2

Printed by McCorquodale Scotland Ltd, Pollokshaws, Glasgow, Scotland

Covers printed by Spectra Print, Cambuslang, Glasgow, Scotland

INTRODUCTION

This constitution was formulated between 1957-1964 at the behest of Scottish business man and patriot Roland E. Muirhead (1868-1964). His office at Elmbank Crescent, Glasgow was the meeting place of the Committee of Articles whose task it was to examine the constitutions of the world.

The Constitution was still incomplete when the Scottish Constituent Provisional Assembly convened in the George Adam's Ballroom in Edinburgh on April 21st 1962 when one hundred and eight delegates turned up to hold Scotland's first Assembly since 1707.

Throughout the seven years of the making of the Constitution, the Public and the Media were consulted step by step in order to legalise the Constitution.

The ninety seven articles enable every facet of government in Scotland to be covered. With this legal constitution, a democratically elected Scottish government can direct the Executive, the Police, the Armed Forces, Internal Security, Foreign Policy and Domestic Spending.

The finest legal brains in Scotland helped write this Constitution, legal men and women who gave freely of their busy professional lives to ensure Scotland's place amongst the nation's of the world. The late Professor Andrew Dewar Gibb, Chair of Scots Law Glasgow University, Dr.Victor S. MacKinnon, Lecturer in Constitutional Law Edinburgh University and other legal notables of their day gave endless advice and criticism to the Constitutional Committee workers Somerville, Snodgrass and MacLean who drafted the constitution into its finished form.

Throughout the long years of research, these men and women of the legal profession ensured that the people of Scotland in the future would manage their own affairs and live in harmony with the rest of the world.

John Murphy, Delegate, 1962 Scottish Assembly

Glasgow, 6th April 1993

This publication is dedicated to the memory of Roland Eugene Muirhead who for seventy five years relentlessly campaigned for an independent Scottish parliament.

ARTICLE 1 : Scotland is a free, independent, democratic nation, the power to rule being vested in the Scottish people and exercised by them through a National Assembly appointed by a free vote of its citizens.

ARTICLE 2 : All persons who were domiciled in Scotland at the time of the promulgation of this Constitution shall be citizens of Scotland. Thereafter the acquisition of and loss of Scottish citizenship shall be determined by law, but no person who is a citizen of any other country can be citizen of Scotland except in cases where the National Assembly by an unanimous resolution shall confer Honorary Citizenship.

ARTICLE 3 : Scotland is, in territory, all the mainland, islands, and territorial seas which are subject to the jurisdiction of the Scottish Courts. The capital city of Scotland is the City of Edinburgh.

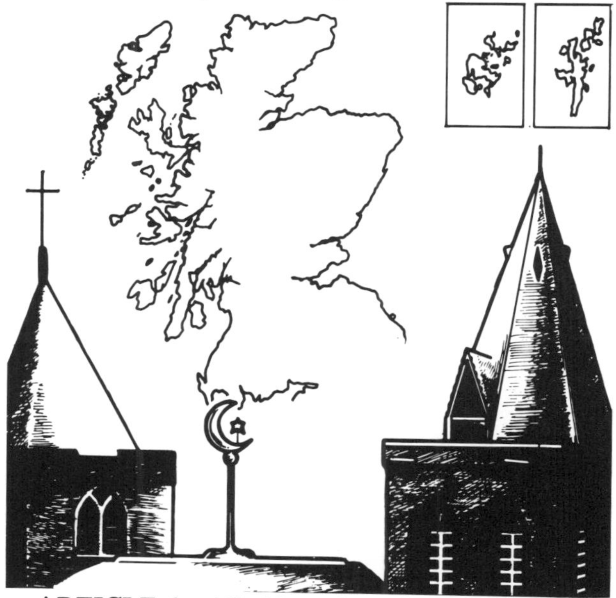

ARTICLE 4 : All citizens have freedom of religious belief and worship and there shall be no discrimination on grounds of religion. The national church is the Church of Scotland by law defined in the Act for Securing the Protestant Religion and Presbyterian Church Government in the Kingdom of Scotland, 1707, and the Acts Declaratory of the Constitution of the Church of Scotland in Matters Spiritual, 1921.

ARTICLE 5 : The defence of the territory of the nation, its institutions and general safety, is the duty of every citizen, but no citizen shall bear arms unless called upon and authorised to do so by laws enacted by the National Assembly.

ARTICLE 6 : The land and natural resources of the nation shall be fully developed and utilized in the interest of the commonweal. The extent of individual and corporate ownership of land and natural resources shall be limited by law, and all monopolies shall be regulated by the National Assembly.

ARTICLE 7 : In the event of the business of a trading, manufacturing, industrial, or any other company domiciled in Scotland being offered for sale, there shall be a right of pre-emption in the National Assembly if the proposed purchaser is a foreign person or concern situated or domiciled furth of Scotland, and provided always that the price offered by the National Assembly shall, in the opinion of independent experts to be summoned, be a fair price.

ARTICLE 8 : The state shall protect the basic natural institution of society of which the chief are marriage and the family.

ARTICLE 9 : The state shall provide social services for the maintenance of the health, education, and general well-being of the people.

ARTICLE 10 : The state shall take all possible steps to safeguard the cultural heritage of the nation and shall initiate such measures as are within its power to foster the arts and to promote the full cultural life of the people.

ARTICLE 11 : Every citizen shall be liable to pay a share of public expenses in the form of taxes and other dues.

INLAND
REVENUE

ARTICLE 12 : The National Flag is the White Saltire on Azure Blue: the National Badge is the Thistle proper: the Motto is "Nemo me impune lacessit": the Ensign of Public Authority is the Sovereign Achievement (Royal Arms) of Scotland undifferenced: the Great Seal of Scotland shall bear the Sovereign Achievement (Royal Arms) of Scotland undifferenced: the Royal Banner in use in Scotland shall be the tressured Lion Rampant: all as recorded in the Register of Arms by the Lyon King of Arms.

ARTICLE 13 : The state is not omnipotent, it exists solely to serve the commonweal. At all times, in all its agencies, it shall remain the servant of the citizens and shall be subservient to their fundamental rights as set forth in this Constitution. The state shall not violate the person or the liberty of the individual, nor shall any individual be deprived of personal liberty or property save by due process of law.

Local Surgeries

Every Tues 7.30pm in the Town Hall rooms

Monday and Thurs 6.30pm in Municipal Library

ARTICLE 14 : All citizens are equal in rights and obligations and are equal before the law. The right of Gaelic-speaking citizens to use their mother tongue before the Courts and the administrative authorities, and to obtain from them all their publications in Gaelic, shall be guaranteed by law.

BONN 14: Tha còirichean agus dleasdanasan co-ionnan aig luchd-stàit fa chomhair an lagha. Bidh e stèidhichte anns an lagh gu bheil còir aig luchd-stàit a bhruidhneas Gàidhlig an cànan-màthaireil a chleachdadh air beulaibh nan Cùirtean-lagha agus nan roinnean-riaghlach, agus bidh còir aca na clò-bhualaidhean uile aig na buidheannan sin fhaighinn bhuapa ann an Gàidhlig.

ARTICLE 15 : No citizen shall be compelled against his conscience to render service to the state involving the use of force of arms. Exemption from such service shall be regulated by law.

ARTICLE 16: All citizens shall have the right of freedom of expression and of dissemination of opinion by speech, by writing, and by all visual and auditory media, and the right of free access to information from generally available sources. Freedom of the press, radio, television, the theatre, motion pictures, and all other forms of general communication shall be limited only by law, and for such causes as the law may define.

ARTICLE 17 : There shall be no official censorship save in the case of serious emergency under an Emergency Measures Act whose duration shall be limited to a maximum period of 12 months, but subject to renewal by the National Assembly.

ARTICLE 18 : All citizens shall have the right of peaceable assembly.

ARTICLE 19 : All citizens shall have the right to form associations and societies except where the objects or activities of such associations or societies conflict with the law.

ARTICLE 20 : No citizen shall be forced to follow a specific trade or profession or to enter a place of training or a place of work against his or her will, except when deprived of his or her liberty after due process of law. No citizen shall be compelled, as a condition of his right to work, to join, or to abstain from joining, any society, association or combination.

ARTICLE 21 : Secrecy of the mail and telecommunications shall be inviolable. Restrictions may be ordered only by law.

ARTICLE 22 : Every citizen has the right to leave the country at any time. This right may be restricted only on a warrant issued by a Sheriff.

ARTICLE 23 : The home shall not be violated. Searches may be ordered only by a Sheriff or, in the event of danger in delay, by other agents as provided by law, and may be carried out only in the form and manner prescribed by law. The right of people to be secure in their persons, premises, papers, and effects, against searches and seizures, shall not be violated, except on a warrant issued by a Sheriff.

ARTICLE 24 : Every citizen when charged with a breach of the law shall be presumed innocent until his or her guilt has been proven in a court of law.

ARTICLE 25 : No citizen shall be detained in custody longer than 48 hours before being brought before a court of law and charged with a breach of the law. The trial of every person who has been charged and detained in prison, or remanded on bail, must be completed within a period of 110 days from the date on which he or she was committed, except, as heretofore, in case of emergency.

7 14 21 28 35
42 49 56 63
70 77 84 91
98 105 110

ARTICLE 26 : In the event of the infringement of any of the aforementioned fundamental rights, or of any recognised Common Law right, a citizen can seek redress at law, or by submitting a personal petition to the Commissioner of Commonweal, as provided in Article 65 hereof.

ARTICLE 27: The constitutional head of state is the King or Queen, if Queen regnant, deriving title from the Act of Settlement, 1700, and the Treaty of Union, 1707, hereinafter referred to as the Sovereign.

ARTICLE 28: The Sovereign is proclaimed King or Queen, at Mercat Cross of Edinburgh, on the death or abdication of the reigning Sovereign.

ARTICLE 29: The Sovereign shall be crowned King or Queen of Scots with the Scottish Crown in Edinburgh.

ARTICLE 30: The Sovereign on Coronation shall take an oath to uphold entire the Constitution of the Kingdom of Scotland.

ARTICLE 31: No office of state can be held by any person who is not a citizen of Scotland, except as provided in the Special Provisions of this Constitution.

ARTICLE 32: The Representative of the Sovereign in Scotland shall be the Sovereign's Commissioner and shall be styled the King's or Queen's Commissioner; he or she shall be appointed by the Sovereign on the advice of the Executive Council, provided for in Article 45 hereof, for a term of five years. The appointment of the Sovereign's Commissioner can be terminated, or his or her resignation accepted by the Sovereign, before the full term of office has expired, on the advice of the Executive Council.

ARTICLE 33: The functions of the Sovereign shall be exercised by the Sovereign or the Sovereign's Commissioner solely and always on the advice of the Executive Council.

Following a meeting of the National Executive, it was unanimously agreed that a state visit to Iceland would be in the interest of closer relations between our two nations.

APPROVED by EXECUTIVE COUNCIL

ARTICLE 34: The Sovereign shall summon, prologue and dissolve the parliaments of the National Assembly.

ARTICLE 35: The Sovereign shall address the National Assembly at the opening of each session of parliament, and on the invitation of the National Assembly.

ARTICLE 36: The power of pardoning for crime shall reside in the Sovereign who shall act on the advice of the Commissioner of Commonweal.

ARTICLE 37: The power to appoint ambassadors, to declare war and to make treaties, shall reside in the Sovereign, and shall be exercised solely on the advice of the Executive Council.

SOVEREIGN P
TREA

The proviso at the end of the article distinguishes a constitutional head of state from

ARTICLE 38: The Sovereign or the Sovereign's Commissioner, shall grant, in Edinburgh, credentials to the diplomatic representatives of Scotland, and shall receive, in Edinburgh, the credentials of the official representatives of other nations accredited to him or her as the Sovereign of the Scots.

ARTICLE 39: The Sovereign, and the Sovereign's Commissioner, shall have official residencies in Edinburgh

ARTICLE 40: The Sovereign shall confer decorations for distinguished services only on the advice, or with the consent, of the National Assembly. No rank or title shall be conferred other than that which each office carries with it. The title *Lord* shall cease to be used in relation to all offices within the nation. No personal or hereditary titles or privileges shall be recognised other than those of Princes and Princesses of the blood royal within the immediate succession. There shall be no party-political honours or decorations. No citizen shall accept rank, title, or privilege from the head of any other state or from the government of any other state without first securing the sanction of the National Assembly. Awards for humane achievements may be awarded and accepted without sanctions.

ARTICLE 41: The chief secretary of state and head of the Executive Council of the National Assembly shall be styled the Prime Minister. He shall be nominated by the National Assembly and appointed to his office by the Sovereign who shall also receive his resignation. The Prime Minister at the time of his nomination must be a member of the National Assembly.

ARTICLE 42: The executive and administrative functions of the National Assembly shall be exercised through departments of state. The number, responsibilities, and functions of such departments shall be established by law.

ARTICLE 43: Each department of state shall be in charge of a Secretary of State who shall be appointed and whose resignation shall be received by the Sovereign on the advice of the Prime Minister. Each Secretary must be a member of the National Assembly.

Secretary of Education

ARTICLE 44: The Prime Minister and Secretaries of State shall be, individually and jointly, responsible to the National Assembly which shall have the power to call to account and to censure the Prime Minister and any Secretary of State. If a motion of no confidence in the Executive Council is passed by a majority of five members of the National Assembly, present and voting, the Executive Council shall resign as a body.

ARTICLE 45: The Prime Minister and such Secretaries of State as may be provided for by law - the following always being included, the Secretary of State for Home Affairs, Foreign Affairs, Health and Welfare, Education, Defence, Scientific and Economic Development, and the Treasury - shall form the Executive Council of the National Assembly. The Prime Minister shall reside over the Executive Council.

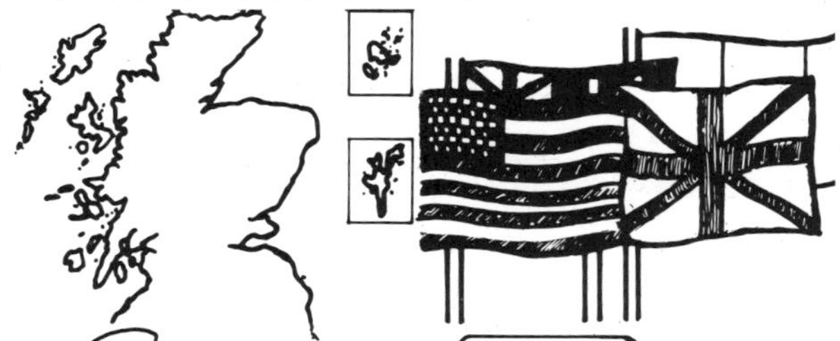

ARTICLE 46: The Prime Minister, Secretaries for State, and the President of the National Assembly shall receive such remuneration as shall from time to time be provided by Act of the National Assembly.

EXECUTIVE OFFICERS SALARIES

PRIME MINISTER ================ £xx,xxx

SECRETARY - TREASURY ========== £xx,xxx

SECRETARY - HOME AFFAIRS ====== £xx,xxx

ARTICLE 47: The executive Council shall have powers of inquiry and may, with the approval of the National Assembly, appoint special commissions with powers of summons to investigate and report to the National Assembly on matters of general or specific importance. The Prime Minister of any Secretary of State shall not have sole power to appoint any tribunal of investigation or any commission of inquiry of any kind.

ARTICLE 48: The Sovereign, or the Sovereign's Commissioner, shall be informed in general terms by the Prime Minister of the decisions of the Executive Council, but neither of them shall be present at its deliberations.

ARTICLE 49: Bills passed by the National Assembly which have been given the Sovereign's assent, or the assent of the Sovereign's Commissioner on his or her behalf, shall become laws of Scotland; the only Bills which shall not require the Sovereign's assent shall be the bills to amend the Constitution : these having been passed by the National Assembly shall be submitted to a National referendum, as provided for in Article 97 hereof.

This Bill is not an amendment to the Constitution and requires the assent of the Sovereign.

APPROVED

ARTICLE 50: The people of Scotland shall exercise legislative power through the National Assembly, whose members shall be styled Commissioners.

ARTICLE 51: The seat of the National Assembly shall be Edinburgh. In exceptional circumstances, the Assembly may meet in other places in Scotland.

ARTICLE 52: The National Assembly shall be elected by direct universal suffrage by secret ballot, in accordance with methods and conditions laid down by Acts of the National Assembly.

ARTICLE 53: The system used for electing Commissioners shall be Proportional Representation by the Single Transferable Vote.

AHMED, Callum (Red Party)	2
PETERS, Heather (White Party)	1
KENNEDY, Lynda	3
WALLACE, Robert (Blue Party)	4

ARTICLE 54: The right of voting shall belong to every citizen who has attained the age of 18 years, is of legal capacity and is not a convicted criminal in custody.

ARTICLE 55: The number of Commissioners of the National Assembly shall from time to time be fixed by law, but the total number of Commissioners shall not be fixed at less than one Commissioner for each 25,000 electors. The ratio between the number of Commissioners to be elected at any one time for each constituency and the population of each constituency, as ascertained at the last preceding census, shall as far as is practicable, be the same throughout the country.

National Assembly

ELECTION OF COMMISSIONER RETURNS

AHMED, Callum (Red Party)	6,254
PETERS, Heather (White Party)	11,561
KENNEDY, Lynda	4,386
WALLACE, Robert (Blue Party)	2,799
Electoral Turnout	100%

Heather Peters is duly elected to the National Assembly

ARTICLE 56: Every candidate for election as a Commissioner to the National Assembly must be a citizen of Scotland over 21 years of age, who has the right to vote and who is not an undischarged bankrupt, or a person who has standing against him or her an unpaid fine for a criminal offence.

ARTICLE 57: The National Assembly is elected for a term of four years, but a General Election may be held before the expiry of the full term, by a decision of the National Assembly on a motion submitted by at least 25 Commissioners and supported by a majority of five members of the National Assembly present and voting. The date of each General Election shall be decided by the National Assembly.

ARTICLE 58: Each duly elected Commissioner to the National Assembly must make and subscribe a solemn declaration that he or she will uphold the Constitution before becoming eligible to take his or her seat.

ARTICLE 59: The National Assembly must seat a Commissioner duly elected in accordance with the provisions of the Constitution and the electoral laws, and who makes the declaration of adherence (Art.58). Each Commissioner shall be bound to conform to such rules of procedure as the National Assembly shall from time to time establish.

ARTICLE 60: A Commissioner cannot be arrested, or cited civilly, or tried for opinions or comment expressed, or for statements made, or for activities undertaken, in pursuance of his duties within the National Assembly. This immunity does not extend to a Commissioner in breach of Criminal Law.

ARTICLE 61: A Commissioner can only be deprived of his or her seat during his or her elected term, if convicted of a criminal offence specified in the Rules of the National Assembly.

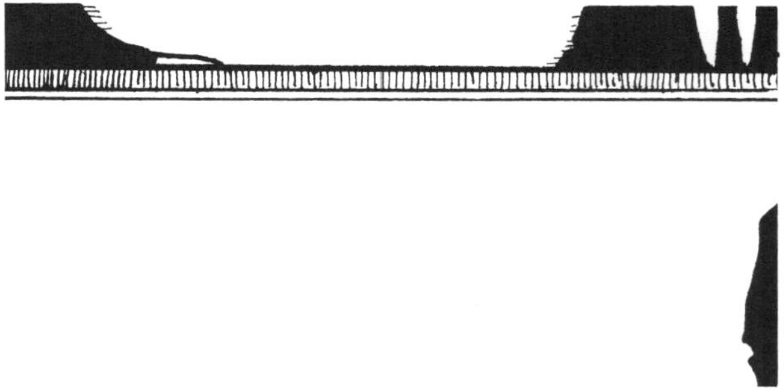

ARTICLE 62: Each Commissioner on taking his or her seat in the National Assembly shall receive such remuneration and expenses as shall be determined by the National Assembly which shall organise office accommodation and secretarial services for each Commissioner.

COMMISSIONER'S EXPENSES

National Assembly Accomm ============= £x,xxx

Secretarial Assistance ================= £xx,xxx

If a Commissioner is to do his or her work properly he or she should have a place of their own (an office) in the precincts of the National Assembly. Secretarial help is necessary if a Commissioner is to maintain a

ARTICLE 63: The National Assembly shall exercise the legislative power of the nation in relation to, but not restricted to, the following :-

(a) the imposition of taxes, duties, customs and other public charges; (b) the control of the finances of the nation, securing loans on the credit of the nation and appropriating the sums of money necessary to meet the expenditure of the state; (c) the determination of the annual appropriation for the Sovereign's privy purse and Royal Household and for the annual honorarium of the Sovereign's Commissioner in Scotland; (d) the revision of the list of official salaries and pensions. (e) It shall have laid before it the complete records of the Executive Council including all documents. (f) It shall have powers of summons and inquiry in matters of state. (g) It shall nominate and appoint an Auditor General who shall, annually, examine the accounts of the state and publish a report thereon, and provide for the organisation of an office wherein such audits can be undertaken. (h) It shall grant naturalisation and citizenship rights.

ARTICLE 64: The National Assembly shall adhere to the procedures set forth in this Constitution for the making of the laws. In a case of serious emergency under an Emergencies Measures Act the National Assembly may delegate legislative power to the Executive Council, as in Article 17 hereof.

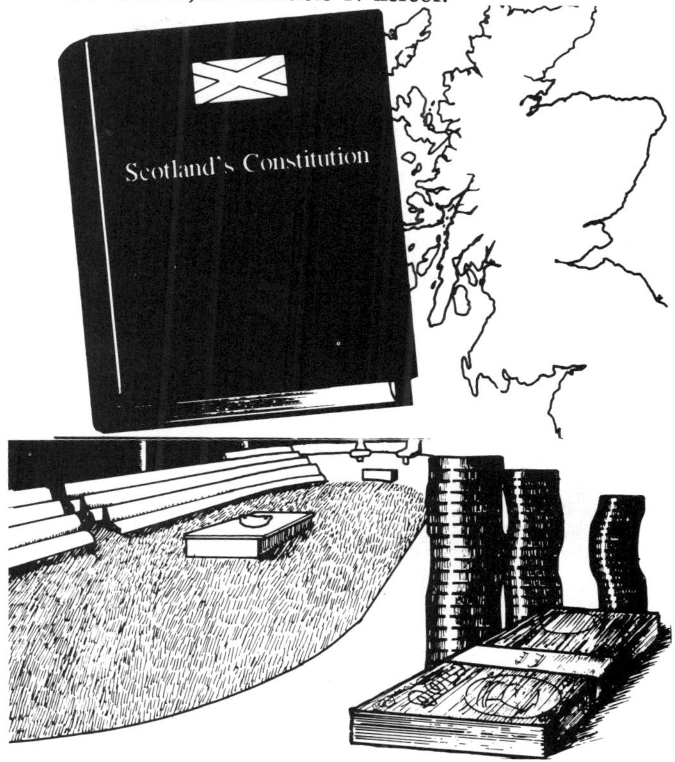

ARTICLE 65 : The National Assembly shall appoint a citizen of legal education, qualification and ability and of known personal integrity as a Commissioner for Administration who shall be styled Commissioner of Commonweal, to supervise, on behalf of the National Assembly, all central and local government administration.

The Commissioner of Commonweal shall be appointed one month after each General Election and shall continue in office until one month after the next General Election when he shall be eligible for reappointment by the National Assembly for a further term. He shall :

(a) keep under review the effects on the citizens of the application of laws and statutes:

(b) receive by petition all complaints of injustices and infringements of private and fundamental rights alleged to have been committed by, or caused by the negligence or mistake of, the National or Local Government Authorities, administration, or agencies, or any of their servants, against the petitioner :

(c) be accorded full powers of investigation, including unreserved access to all records and correspondence, and the right to cite witnesses :

(d) cause to be brought to Court any case requiring legal judgement, or call on a Government Department or Local Authority to take disciplinary or other appropriate action.

A Deputy Commissioner of Commonweal, having the same qualities as the Commissioner, may be appointed under the same conditions and for a similar term of office.

The Commissioner of Commonweal shall be accorded the salary of a Judge of the Court of session and shall be granted an appropriate pension. He shall not hold any office in public or private companies, enterprises, or institutions, except with the consent of a committee which the National Assembly shall instruct to decide on this question.

The Commissioner of Commonweal of the deputy Commissioner of Commonweal shall not be removed from office before the expiry of his or her full term except for conduct repugnant to his or her office or for physical or mental incapacity, and then only on a decision of three-quarters of the total membership of the National Assembly.

The duties of the Commissioner of Commonweal shall be laid down in general terms by the National Assembly, but subject to these provision he or she shall be independent of the National Assembly in the performance of his or her duties.

The Commissioner of Commonweal's jurisdiction shall comprise Secretaries of State, Civil Servants, and persons acting in the service of the state or local government, but shall not include any court of law superior to the courts of local magistrates.

The Commissioner of Commonweal shall present to the National Assembly an Annual Report in which he or she shall give an account of the administration of the affairs of state, and he shall draw the attention of the national Assembly to defects in the working of existing laws and statutes. The Report shall be printed and published.

ARTICLE 66: Except when determined by a General Election the parliamentary sessions of the National Assembly shall commence on the first Tuesday in October and end on the Monday preceding the first Tuesday in October in the following year. Meetings shall be held regularly during at least eight months of each session. The number and hours of meetings and the dates and duration of the recess shall be determined by the National Assembly and set forth as statutory provisions.

OCTOBER

TUESDAY 5TH!

ARTICLE 67: The National Assembly shall be presided over by a President who shall be elected from the Commissioners to the National Assembly at the first meeting of the first parliament after every General Election. The President shall be the constitutional representative of the National Assembly.

He or she shall exercise their office with complete objectivity and impartiality and in accordance with the Rules of Procedure. He or she shall retain their office from the date of their election until the next General Election after which he or she shall be seated as a Commissioner in the new National Assembly without having submitted him or herself to the electorate. He or She shall be eligible for re-election to the office of President.

The President shall be responsible for the effective functioning of the National Assembly and shall exercise domestic authority through a House Committee and shall be controller of the administrative officials and employees of the Assembly. A Vice-President shall also be elected to assist the President and to act as his deputy as and when required.

ARTICLE 68: In the first week of each parliamentary session the Sovereign shall open the proceedings of the National Assembly informing it of the general state of the nation and of the legislative programme of the executive council

ARTICLE 69: This speech shall be the subject of a general debate following the withdrawal of the Sovereign.

ARTICLE 70: The President of the National Assembly shall preside over all meetings of the Assembly.

ARTICLE 71: Any Commissioner of the Assembly shall be entitled to introduce Bills and other Measures but the legislative programme and order of business shall be arranged by the President and a Bills Committee of the National Assembly from the Bills and Measures submitted by the Executive Council and by Commissioners.

In allocating times and priorities, the submissions of the Executive Council shall take precedence, but a quarter of the time of each session must be reserved for the Commissioners' Bills and Measures. Where this provision is not fully utilized, the balance of time may be taken up by Executive Bills and Measures. Conversely, any balance of time outstanding from the submissions of the Executive Council may be taken up by Commissioners' Bills and measures.

ARTICLE 72 : No Bill or Measure shall be finally passed for Royal assent until it has been read three times in the National Assembly and passed by a simple majority of the National Assembly.

After the first reading and before the second all Bills and measures before the National Assembly may be submitted for scrutiny and comment to the Constitutional Court of the realm, as provided in Article 84 hereof. The Constitutional Court shall return all Bills and measures so submitted, along with its comments thereon, not later than ten days from the date of their submission.

Two-fifths of the Commissioners of the National Assembly present and voting may request the President that the third reading of the Bill or Measure should be deferred for a period of two weeks after the passing of the second reading. This request must be made in writing and signed by the Commissioners making it.

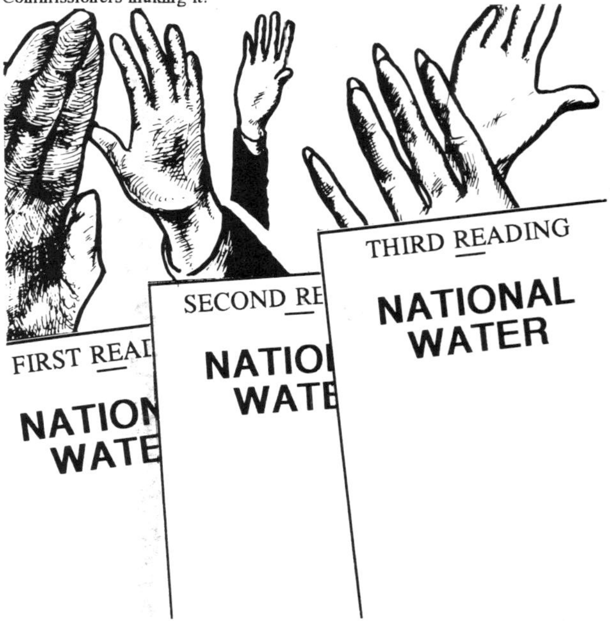

ARTICLE 73: The National Assembly shall lay down its own Rules of Procedure, including rules governing its conduct of business and maintenance of order.

ARTICLE 74: The sessions of the parliaments of the National Assembly shall be conducted in public at all times. Secret sessions can only be held on matters concerning national security and then only by a majority agreement of the Commissioners of the National Assembly. The proceedings of the National Assembly shall be published verbatim every week, the only exceptions being the minutes of secret sessions, these minutes, however, shall be available on request to all Commissioners of the National Assembly.

ARTICLE 75: Commissioners shall have the right to ask questions of the Prime Minister and any Secretary of State, and, with the approval of the National Assembly, to receive both written and spoken answers.

ARTICLE 76: Save as hereinafter declared the judicial power in Scotland shall be exercised in the same Courts with the same jurisdiction and by the same Judges having the same powers, duties, immunity, and privileges as at the date of promulgation of this Constitution, and except on special cause shewn justice shall always be administered in public.

ARTICLE 77: There shall be created a Council of Judiciary to advise the Sovereign on certain judicial appointments. The Council shall consist of eleven members, five Senators of the College of Justice and five Commissioners of the National Assembly who shall appoint their own Chairman. The Chairman shall not be a member of the legal profession or a Commissioner of the National Assembly or an official or an executive or council member of any political party.

ARTICLE 78: The power to appoint Judges of the Court of Session and Commissioners of Justiciary shall reside in the Sovereign who shall act on the advice of the Council of Judiciary as provided in Article 77 hereof.

Council of Judiciary
Recommendation

In light of the recent retirement of Judge Scott due to il health, the Council of Justiciary recommends to the Sovereign the appointment of John Black as a Judge of the Court of Session.

APPROVED

ARTICLE 79: The power to appoint Sheriff Principals and Sheriff Substitutes shall reside in the Sovereign who shall act on the advice of the Council of Judiciary. These judges shall be called respectively ''Principal Sheriffs'' and ''Sheriffs Depute.''

ARTICLE 80: The power to appoint Justices of the Peace shall reside in and be exercised by the President of the Court of session, who shall have power to remove them for misconduct in their office.

ARTICLE 81: The jurisdiction of the Court of session shall be exercised in the same manner as at the time of the promulgation of this Constitution and the Court shall have originating and appellate functions, but the decisions of the Inner House shall be final. There shall be created a Court of Criminal Appeal which shall be composed of Commissioners of Justiciary who are not members of the High Court of Justiciary. The decisions of the Court of Criminal Appeal shall be final.

ARTICLE 82: The power of prosecution shall reside exclusively in the Advocate General and the Solicitor General and their subordinates and the right of private prosecution shall be abolished.

ARTICLE 83: The appointment of the Advocate General and the Solicitor General shall reside in the Sovereign who shall act on the advice of the Senators of the College of Justice.

College of Justice
Senator's Guidelines

The appointment of Lord Advocate or Advocate-General shall made on grounds of professional competence and esteem and not on a party political basis. The procedure to be followed in deciding what advice is to be given to the Sovereign shall be laid down by Act of the National Assembly.

ARTICLE 84: There shall be created a Constitutional Court of the Realm. The jurisdiction of the Constitutional Court shall cover : (a) all questions of the validity of any law enacted by the national Assembly: (b) any infringement of the Constitution: (c) disputes concerning the constitutional assignment of powers and the exercise of powers within the state.

ARTICLE 85: The Constitutional Court of the Realm shall comprise the Senators of the College of Justice sitting as a Collegiate body; seven Senators shall form a quorum.

ARTICLE 86: Any individual citizen or group or association of citizens whether official or unofficial shall have the constitution right to raise in the Constitutional Court any issue which they believe comes within the competence of the Court.

ARTICLE 87: The jurisdiction of the Court of Session, of the High Court of Justiciary, or any inferior court whatever, shall not extend to the question of the constitutional validity of the law or of any provision of the law.

ARTICLE 88: Every person appointed to exercise a judicial function under the Constitution shall make and subscribe a declaration that he or she will uphold the Constitution and the law.

ARTICLE 89: All Judges shall be independent in the exercise of their judicial functions and subject only to the Constitution and the law.

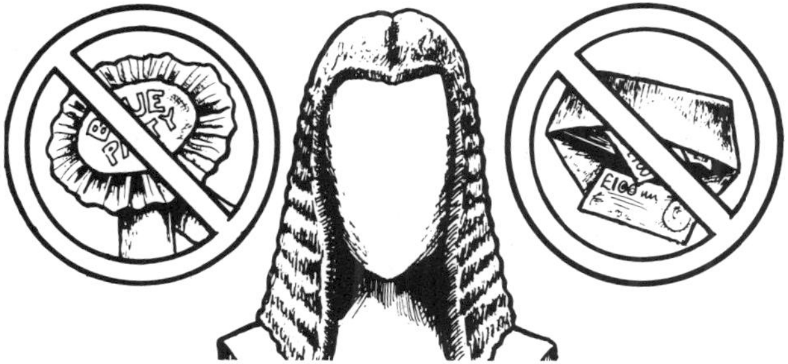

ARTICLE 90: No person exercising a judicial function shall be eligible to be a Commissioner of the National Assembly or to hold other office or position of emolument.

ARTICLE 91: Judges of the Court of Session, Commissioners of Judiciary and Sheriffs shall not be removed from office except for conduct repugnant to their office, or for physical or mental incapacity, and then only by an address from the National Assembly assented to by three quarters of the Commissioners of the National Assembly.

ARTICLE 92: The National Assembly shall grant to Local Authorities certain rights and powers to make and publish local bylaws and to levy local rates and taxes and to manage their own affairs. All such rights and powers shall be safeguarded by law, but all bylaws and levies shall be subject to the scrutiny and sanction of the National Assembly.

ARTICLE 93: The areas and functions of Local Authorities shall be defined by statute in such a manner as to provide local bodies with as much power and initiative as is practicable within the Constitution.

ARTICLE 94: During the first four years after the promulgation of this Constitution persons over 21 years of age who were born and educated in Scotland but who are domiciled furth of Scotland shall be eligible for appointment to office in the service of the state provided that they take up residence and become domiciled in Scotland immediately on appointment to such office. Such persons on appointment, shall, along with their dependents, become citizens of Scotland.

ARTICLE 95: During the first year after the promulgation of this Constitution persons over 21 years of age who were born and educated in Scotland but who are domiciled furth of Scotland may stand for election as Commissioners of the National Assembly at the first general election to be held after the promulgation of this Constitution, provided that they have taken up residence and become domiciled in Scotland. On being nominated for election such persons and their dependents shall become citizens of Scotland.

ARTICLE 96: During the first decade after the promulgation of this Constitution it shall be the duty of successive National Assemblies to apply in any casus improvisus the law which has hitherto applied and as early as possible to introduce a measure for remedying the defect. It shall furthermore be the duty of successive National Assemblies to appoint a Commission of the Constitution to make recommendations for correcting discernible defects.

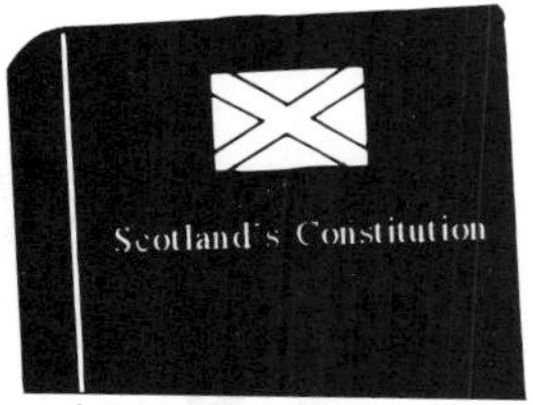

AMENDMENTS

1. Land is the common property of all Scots.
2. Whatever a Scot produces from his or her own labour is the private property of that Scot.
3. Each generation has full title to a free Scotland in which the land is the

ARTICLE 97: The articles of this Constitution can be amended, whether by modification, addition, or repeal, only in accordance with the following provisions:-

(a) each proposal for an amendment shall be initiated in the National Assembly as a Bill and shall be published in print:

(b) such a Bill having been passed by a two-thirds majority of the total membership of the National Assembly shall be submitted by Referendum to the decision of the electorate in accordance with laws governing the conduct of a Referendum which shall be passed by the National Assembly;

(c) each proposal for amendment of this Constitution which is submitted by Referendum to the decision of the electorate shall be held to have been approved by the electorate, if, upon having been submitted, a simple majority of votes cast at such a Referendum shall have been cast in favour of its enactment into law;

(d) every such Bill shall be entitled "A Bill to Amend the Constitution";

(e) a Bill containing a proposal for the amendment of this Constitution having been passed by the National Assembly and approved by the electorate in a Referendum in accordance with the provisions of this Article (97) shall become a part of the Constitution.

Thus ends the Ninety Seven Articled Constitution of Scotland designed to help the people of Scotland to move forward to an independent future.

ACKNOWLEDGEMENTS

The publishers would like to thank the following for their contribution to this publication:

John Murphy, delegate 1962 Scottish Assembly, for original typescript

Hugh MacDiarmid, delegate 1962 Scottish Assembly, for backcover quotation

Derick S. Thomson, professor retired, Glasgow University, for Gaelic translation

Paul Bonatti, Media Stills Photography, for artwork reproduction

Lynda Latus, Latus Publishing, for sales and publicity

Chris Kennedy, for marketing and sales help

W.D.Brown, Thurso, for encouragement and financial contribution

Freedom Magazine, in which part of an early version of this work appeared